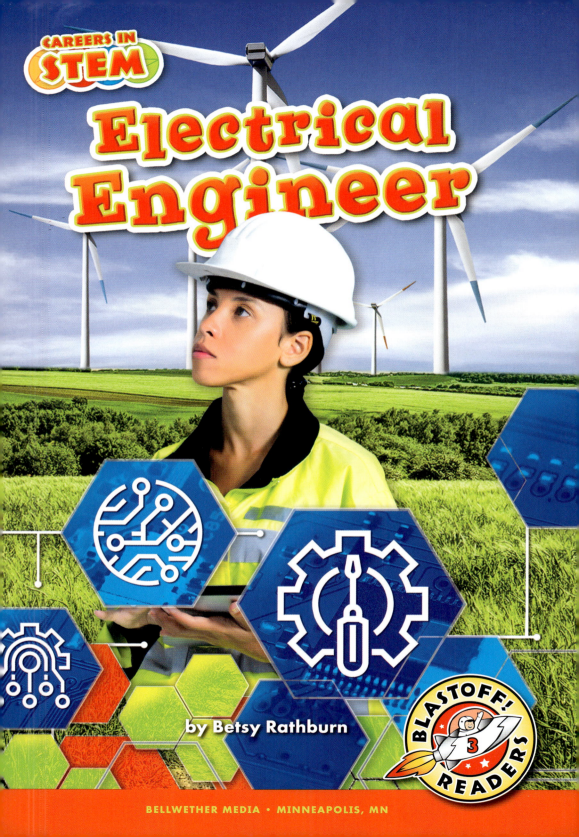

Blastoff! Readers are carefully developed by literacy experts to build reading stamina and move students toward fluency by combining standards-based content with developmentally appropriate text.

 Level 1 provides the most support through repetition of high-frequency words, light text, predictable sentence patterns, and strong visual support.

 Level 2 offers early readers a bit more challenge through varied sentences, increased text load, and text-supportive special features.

 Level 3 advances early-fluent readers toward fluency through increased text load, less reliance on photos, advancing concepts, longer sentences, and more complex special features.

★ **Blastoff! Universe**

Reading Level

Grade K → Grades 1–3 → Grade 4

This edition first published in 2023 by Bellwether Media, Inc.

No part of this publication may be reproduced in whole or in part without written permission of the publisher. For information regarding permission, write to Bellwether Media, Inc., Attention: Permissions Department, 6012 Blue Circle Drive, Minnetonka, MN 55343.

Library of Congress Cataloging-in-Publication Data

LC record for Electrical Engineer available at: https://lccn.loc.gov/2022036399

Text copyright © 2023 by Bellwether Media, Inc. BLASTOFF! READERS and associated logos are trademarks and/or registered trademarks of Bellwether Media, Inc.

Editor: Elizabeth Neuenfeldt   Designer: Andrea Schneider

Printed in the United States of America, North Mankato, MN.

Table of Contents

Planning Power	4
What Is an Electrical Engineer?	6
At Work	10
Becoming an Electrical Engineer	18
Glossary	22
To Learn More	23
Index	24

Planning Power

An electrical engineer works at her computer. She is **designing** a **wind turbine**.

She plans how its **circuits** will be wired together. The turbine will power many homes when it is built!

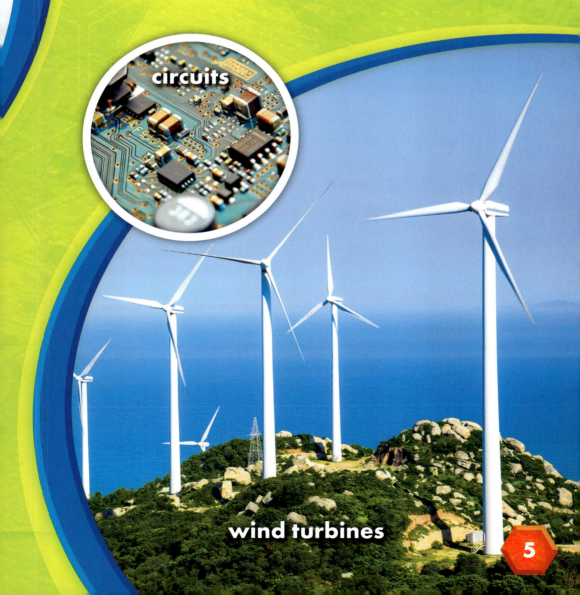

circuits

wind turbines

What Is an Electrical Engineer?

Electrical engineers work with electrical systems. They fix older systems. They make new ones, too.

These systems give power to many kinds of **devices**.

devices

electrical system

Many electrical engineers work for companies. They may work in offices. They may also work at building sites.

Famous Electrical Engineer

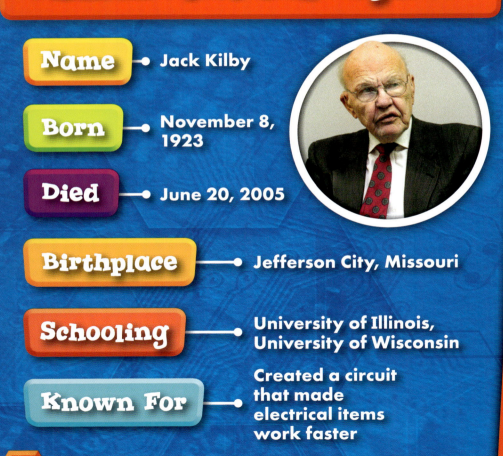

Name: Jack Kilby

Born: November 8, 1923

Died: June 20, 2005

Birthplace: Jefferson City, Missouri

Schooling: University of Illinois, University of Wisconsin

Known For: Created a circuit that made electrical items work faster

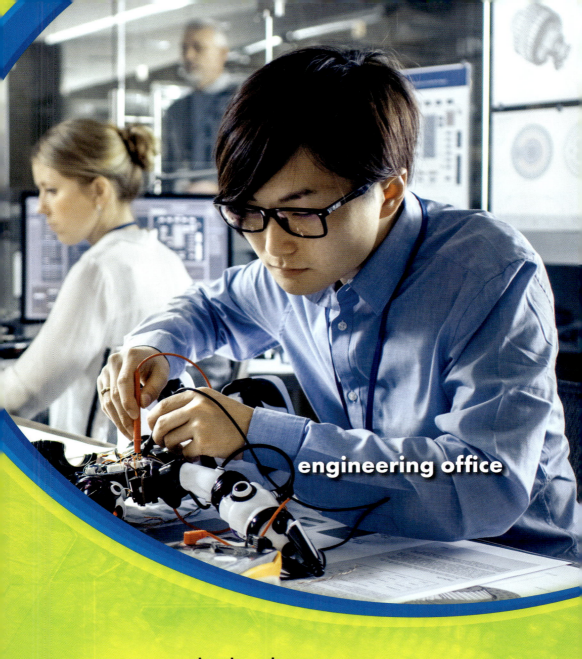

engineering office

Some help the government. They may work on military machines!

At Work

Electrical engineers work on anything that uses electricity! They use computers to design systems.

Some work on **communication** systems. They design **satellites**. They make tools to connect devices to the Internet!

Electrical Engineering in Real Life

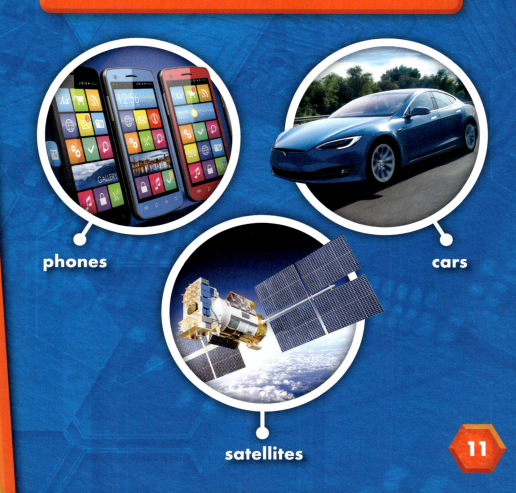

phones

cars

satellites

Some electrical engineers make new devices. They make small items such as phones or TVs.

Others design big machines. They may work on new cars or airplanes!

engineer designing electrical parts for a car

Electrical engineers plan how parts work together. They use **physics** to make sure projects are safe.

They make sure parts are **installed** the right way. Things must be up to **code**.

Using STEM

Science — use physics to make sure projects are safe

Technology — use computers to make designs

Engineering — design electronic devices and machines

Math — figure out how much power projects need

Electrical engineers work with others. They listen to what **customers** want. They make a **schedule**. They plan costs.

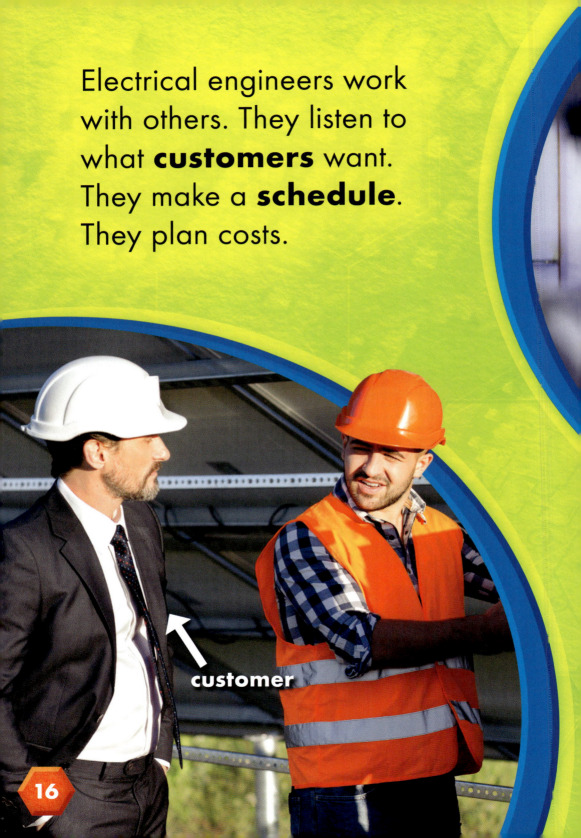

customer

They solve problems. They fix broken systems. They keep things up to date!

Becoming an Electrical Engineer

Electrical engineers study math in college. They also study science. Many study computers, too.

Some learn about **renewable energy**. They make devices that are better for Earth!

renewable energy device

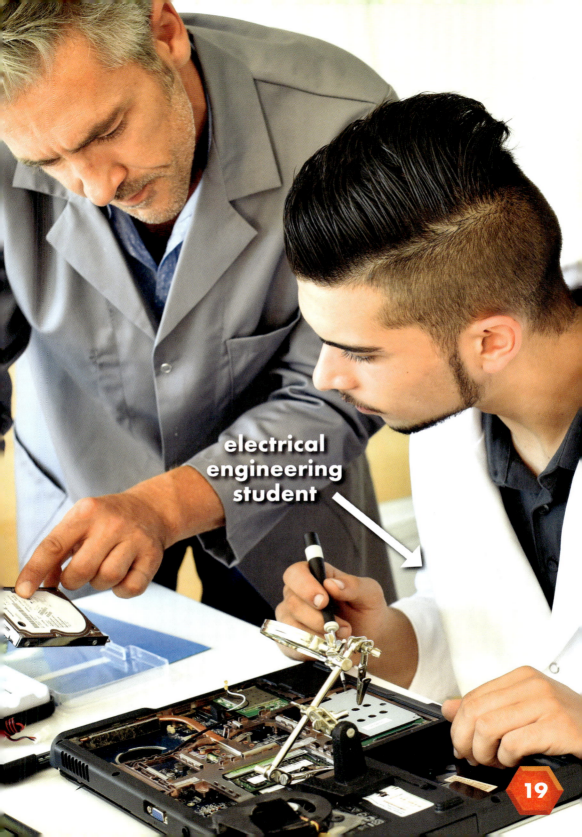

Electrical engineers go to **graduate school**. There, they learn even more. Many get a **license** to work in certain areas.

How to Become an Electrical Engineer

1. study math and science in college

2. go to graduate school

3. find a job

Electrical engineers do important work. They help power the world!

Glossary

circuits—complete paths of electricity

code—a collection of laws

communication—the sharing of information between people

customers—people who buy goods or services

designing—making a plan for a building, object, or pattern

devices—tools that are made for a certain purpose

graduate school—a school where people can study a specialty area after college

installed—put in place for use or service

license—a document that gives electrical engineers permission to work

physics—a science that deals with matter, energy, heat, light, electricity, motion, and sound

renewable energy—energy that does not get used up

satellites—human-made objects that circle Earth; satellites are used to communicate.

schedule—a plan for when things will happen

wind turbine—a large machine that changes wind into electrical energy

To Learn More

AT THE LIBRARY

Noll, Elizabeth. *Computer Programmer*. Minneapolis, Minn.: Bellwether Media, 2023.

Pettiford, Rebecca. *Electricity*. Minneapolis, Minn.: Bellwether Media, 2019.

Sobey, Ed. *Electrical Engineering: Learn It, Try It!* North Mankato, Minn.: Capstone Press, 2018.

ON THE WEB

Factsurfer.com gives you a safe, fun way to find more information.

1. Go to www.factsurfer.com.
2. Enter "electrical engineer" into the search box and click 🔍.
3. Select your book cover to see a list of related content.

Index

building sites, 8
circuits, 5
code, 15
college, 18
companies, 8
computer, 4, 10, 18
costs, 16
customers, 16
designing, 4, 10, 11, 12, 13
devices, 6, 11, 12, 18
Earth, 18
electrical engineering in real life, 11
electrical systems, 6, 7, 10, 11, 17
electricity, 10
government, 9
graduate school, 20
how to become, 20
installed, 15
Internet, 11
Kilby, Jack, 8
license, 20

machines, 9, 12
math, 18
military, 9
offices, 8, 9
parts, 14, 15
physics, 14
power, 5, 6, 21
problems, 17
renewable energy, 18
safe, 14
satellites, 11
schedule, 16
science, 18
turbine, 4, 5
using STEM, 15

The images in this book are reproduced through the courtesy of: Viewfoto studio, front cover (engineer); WDG Photo, front cover (background); Volodymyr Krasyuk, p. 3; Dmytro Zinkevych/ Alamy, pp. 4-5 (engineers); raigvi, p. 5 (circuits); huang yi fri, p. 5 (wind turbines); Oleksiy Mark, pp. 6 (devices), 11 (phones); Kampan, pp. 6-7; Newspaper Member/ AP Images, p. 8 (Jack Kilby); Gorodenkoff, pp. 8-9, 10-11, 12; Abu hasim.A, p. 11 (cars); Andrey Armyagov, p. 11 (satellites); Image Source/ Alamy, pp. 12-13; Chayantorn Tongmorn, pp. 14-15; Zoonar GmbH/ Alamy, p. 16 (customer); Siam Stock, pp. 16-17; Adam Smigielski, p. 18; GOODLUZ/ Alamy, pp. 18-19, 20-21; Suwin Puengsamrong/ Alamy, pp. 20-21 (engineer); Phonlamai Photo, p. 23.